WILD APPLES

Tricia Knoll

Fernwood
PRESS

Wild Apples

poems

©2024 Tricia Knoll

Fernwood Press
Newberg, Oregon
www.fernwoodpress.com

Printed in the United States of America

Cover art: Seraphine de Senlis
Author photo: Kristen D'Agostino

ISBN 978-1-59498-116-6

Dedicated to the loving family I moved away from and the growing family I moved toward.
And the loyal dogs who came along with me.

CONTENTS

ACKNOWLEDGMENTS

Grateful acknowledgment is made to the editors of the journals and anthologies who first published the following poems. The poems, sometimes in earlier versions or with different titles, appeared as follows:

Antiphon: "Advice for the Traveler"

Canary—A Literary Journal of the Environmental Crisis: "Every Day Tell The Hours," "Walking On Water"

Contemporary Haibun Online: "August Night I Sang the Twilight"

Glint Literary Journal: "The Purgatory of Homebound"

Gyroscope Review: "Seduction as Mean as a Snake"

Literary North's blog The Decameron—Stories from the Pandemic, "Messages"

The MacGuffin: "On Loneliness"

Early versions published on the Tupelo Press 30/30 Project (30 poems in 30 days challenge) website in January 2019: "Last Chance New Year's," "Locavore," "Pagan Epiphany in the Night Woods," "Sfumato," "Stolen Color," "Walking on Water"

Playa Residency Anthology: "No Home on the Range"

Randolph, Vermont Poem City celebration of National Poetry

Month, 2021: "Ruth Stone" to hang in the lobby of *The Herald* and "Remainder Snow" to hang in the One Main Tap & Grill en route to a locally published anthology.

Silver Birch Press: "Compass"

The Path to Kindness: Poems of Connection and Joy, "My Daughter Meets My White Pine"

Verse Virtual: "Dropping My Wings Off at Goodwill," "Last Chance—New Years'," "Pagan Epiphany in the Night Woods," "Rhytides," "Rowens," "Knitting is Coding," "September Migration," "The Poetry Writing Handbook for New Years," "Why Buy an Antique Mantel Clock," and "Wild Apples"

Visitant: "Binge Writing," "My impatience is like a fish"

Willawaw Journal: "Why Move?"

Wordgathering—A Journal of Disability Poetry and Literature: "In Praise of Silent Wing"

PREFACE

Minimizing. Downsizing. You start hearing those words in your late sixties. As I turned seventy in 2017, I took a step at downsizing. I rescued a terrier-chihuahua mix of about fourteen pounds. Before that, all my dogs had been big herding dogs, cattle dogs.

I wrote a poem called "I Must Let Go" that contained these lines:

I must let go / of the twenty-five bone china tea cups
and saucers from Germany that my mother used once
in a blue moon at a coffee klatch for women from whom
she hid.

For Thanksgiving 2017, I visited my daughter in Vermont. Wild turkeys raced across pastures. I never saw a traffic jam. Though I had loved living in Oregon for forty-five years, I decided it was time to move 3,003 miles. I had already sold my anchor-house, a small beach cabin on the northern Oregon coast—and wrote *Ocean's Laughter*, a book of poetry about the change over time in this beach-side town, to say good-bye. I was tired of summer's wildfire smoke.

I bought a Vermont house in 2018. More than two feet of snow covered the land—some forest, some pasture, about five acres. The house needed new windows, remediation of mold in one room. My daughter agreed to be the project manager while I finished up in Portland. When the snow melted, she called to say that I didn't own a woods—I'd bought a park. The man who built this house had spent twenty-five years developing his landscape: dozens of rhododendrons, azaleas, hostas, hydrangeas, and more. His choices rested on plants that deer won't eat. I moved my stuff—including those tea cups that summer. For the first time in decades, I would mostly be living alone.

Soon, COVID locked everyone down. Meeting neighbors and getting to know my community was almost impossible. My husband couldn't travel east. What I had was poetry and landscape. A woods. A pasture. Invasive buckthorn and honeysuckle—a workplan of remediation to keep me busy. I connected with the Otter Creek poets of Middlebury for poetry.

Why wild apples? I love New England's rock walls and steam from the sugar shack. I've seen the thermometer plunge below freezing for weeks on end and walked on iced-over ponds. Cardinals and mourning doves hang around my birdfeeders. Here and there, I see twisted apple trees that had once been someone's orchard. Continuing to produce hard apples year after year, content to be untended and which make tart cider.

A metaphor—content to be poet in the woods who wore a mask. Cut off from what I might have yearned for as a larger community. Until two grandsons arrive as blessings.

So, *Wild Apples?* This book's cover image by Seraphine de Senlis—she was an artist who knew bouts of loneliness and sadness. Still, she painted the exuberant oranges and reds of wild fruit trees hung with wild birds. Wild apples beautiful in the hand and tart to the tongue.

12

My Impatience Is Like a Fish

I want to see a star from a high place. Maybe a tree limb, trying not to sway like I have a baby in my arms—my baby is grown up learning to fly fish thousands of miles away from my home. On this lake I visit—where sometimes a loon stops in on clear nights.

Maybe stars guide the fish that wriggle the way I do on a rocking chair on my daughter's dock, tapping my fingers as if wild fish know what goldfish know—that sprinkles of food may fall from waving fingers. As if wiggle above water has meaning.

If I look long enough, maybe the clouds will blow away. Or the loon will come.

Hand Picked

I trust my fingers
to know to pinch off
sprouts of bittercress
before it throws its seeds,

so when I start downsizing,
out goes the Mason jar of mixed
buttons my grandmother snipped
from worn-out clothes.

Next the Madame Alexander doll,
a gift from my mother six decades ago,
what she hoped I might become:
straight-seamed nylons,

feet deformed for strappy heels,
a pink tutu, sky-blue ball gown,
a skirt and blouse for a secretary
to wear to the office.

Her perfect pin-curl hair
is still perfect. Rubber bands
and clips held her head on,
a tight assembly.

A long time ago her head fell off.
In my palm, it weighs as much
as a baseball and smells like closets.
Her torso and legs seem useless—

out they go, and also her clothes.
Though I never gave her a name,
I pack her head to move with me
after stitching white hair from my dog

into her wig so she looks more like me.
She heard the voices I heard.
I lost my head a time or two.
She's not my Yorick; she's my Ruth.

On Loneliness

Are you asking if
you're the only puzzle piece
that fell under the couch?
Absent from its box that's tied up
and ready to recycle?

> *I want to be in a community*
> *the way an aspen leaf holds*
> *a breeze to flip its silver sides.*

L is under-nourished.
Do not feed it anything
that stretches it.
Neither snake oils
nor fake friends.

> *I want to hang onto*
> *where my brother held my hand*
> *walking me to kindergarten.*

Loosen your heart knots.
Braid the best into waterfalls.
Accept a rose, frog,
snowflake, windstorm,
deliveries, or a rock garden
as threads.

> *Let me serve what grows green.*

Hold onto *oneliness*.
Use that loose *L* in other ways:
like mind, live wire
lasting, lavish,
love-make, listen,
laugh, learn, lure, look.

       Let it lighten.

Usually the eagle
hunts alone.
Though not always.

       Fly what is.

Why Move?

Someone had to ask.
From a place as perfect as Oregon.
Vermont has four seasons: freezing,
thaw to mud, bugs, and leaves on fire.

I know trees—
to sniff maple steam in the sugar shack.

To see the wild tom turkey with his harem
high-step over browned-out pasture,
hear the loons moan and trill at Noyes Pond.

As snow tiptoes in on wind, awe here
is rain to skate on.

I can snuggle with a library
moved from Stafford to Frost,
migrate from Tillamook cheese
to Cabot. I believe in creatures
of the deep, Champ.

Vermont is where my daughter is. The girl
who brought home the first deer one fall
when the men drove north to deer camp.
She tagged unblemished roadkill,
freshest deer the butcher ever skinned.

Apron Strings

I never claimed
this coming-of-age gift
from my mother.
Lifted from a drawer,
the blue-and-green calico
goes yellow, the knot she tied.
Her words made promises
of a freedom she could not give.
Now this late-life move,
sorting on her 108th
birthday—the strings
go with me,
the knot still tight.

Dropping My Wings Off at Goodwill

Dust-free, may these soft-gray feathers
fit some other woman's shoulders—

a lonely she looking for a nest,
a lift of loving kindness,
refuge, or to flee
an endangered rest.

The clerk marks them large,
prices them for Halloween,
hangs them on the specials rack
with lipstick-stained wedding gowns
and hand-stitched baby quilts.

She who needs them
may run shaking fingers
to lay the barbs straight.
May she foresee
her whys of flight.

Compass

I'm older than my father was when his heart stopped.
Should I take something that belonged to him?
The mahogany bookends
engraved in Latin or
the pen and ink drawing
of a German forest?
His compass can no longer find north.

I can't leave out his frustration
at trying to teach me to drive,
his joy in our horseback rides
through mountain passes and lush farmland,
that he taught me to swim by throwing me in the lake.
Bike trips and golden dogs.
His chest bared to get a suntan.
His snores in front of the black-
and-white TV, his belief in an apple a day.

The compass does not have to know north.

Memorial Day 2018

This is the day a woman on her knees slathers solvents on stone,
before the man with a power-washer blasts off black swastikas
that bloomed overnight on St. Louis grave markers.

This is the day my friend commits to decorate the graves
of her great-grandparents, good Scots, with red geraniums,
in what was once remote farmland in Yamhill County.

This is the day my Go for Gold rose is forthrightly bold.
Sugar Moon mists its perfume, affirming
my seasons tending. I turn away to head for winters

where hybrid teas do not thrive, where floribundas
and white hydrangeas cluster like moonlit headstones
and the dead accept blankets of snow at remote crossroads.

No Home on that Range

> Our horses neigh to each other
> as we are departing.
> —Li Po

Not homeless, not curled up in cardboard,
old is sold, the new not yet mine.
I float in limbo though the red-wing blackbirds
trill and dust devil of alkali bloom
two stories high across Oregon's playa.

I can smell something
like my father's bay rum,
remember how he'd lift
his chin skyward
so we could admire
the handsome man he was.
I'm going to a place he would love

maybe not as much as this basin land,
where a real cowboy rides a quarter horse
beside a rangy cattle dog to herd steer
from one slope of national forest
to the next. Leaving this West
of greasewood and sage brush
means I let go of the cowgirl.
He would approve holding family close.

Midnight on a Gravel Road

Last night I walked the rutted road
and saw the Milky Way compete
with airplane contrails
and headlights on the highway.
I felt I had to choose.

Last night I walked the black road
and heard the shadows of the does
whisper in pasture grass.
I stopped to sense
I am never all alone.

Last night I walked the dusty road
and inhaled the powder of old rock
that my feet scuffed up
from the scrunch of gravel.
I am of dust.

Last night I walked the winding road,
choosing my footing
around potholes and ruts,
and since the road is in me,
I am not lost.

Advice for the Traveler

Let your lover kiss your arms, cheeks, lips, and neck
for protection. Wash your feet with lavender oil.

Fold pieces of your past
into cranes for your backpack.

Tuck your sliver of a silver saint in a breast pocket.
Double-knot strong laces on generous shoes with hefty tread.

Pull the bill down on your green hat till glory upends it
and the sweat of going gives over to cooler winds.

When a hum rises from the highway, rub whichever bone
is your wishbone and keep on going.

Be not afraid of crosses by the road. Offer them
the gentle roses of your breath.

Verd Mont

As Samuel Champlain wrote on a map in 1647

My Vermont is something like old age wintered-in
until black bears emerge from hibernation hungry,
when ramps carpet the forest floor,
and woodcocks sky dance blurting sexy *bzzts*.

Where the Quebecois buried their siblings
at crossroads under granite stones after thaw
(when serviceberries bloom) and high school classes
explain names like Vergennes, Montpelier, Orleans,
and Grand Isle but not the longevity of poutine
on menus and tourtiere at Christmas.

Feral myths abound around a lake few acknowledge
as the sixth Great Lake—where a woman can walk
out of a fog and never be noticed. One scholar
climbs Hunger Mountain every day to mull
the sayings of Chinese hermits who age as forests do.

This place is almost empty. You learn to drive
without traffic jams to somewhere an hour away to find
people you need, count on plowed roads before noon
and smell cow manure as soon as a thaw sets in.
You accept fly fishing as a varsity sport.

As for climate refugees (burned out, desertified, treading water)
attracted to this land-of-so-few people: owning four winter coats
for gradations of frosty to frigid is reasonable. So is hating ticks.
This was the home of the man who discovered
each snowflake differs from every other one.
We know the muchness of snow.

There is much to love: Morgan horses;
merino wool socks that are Darn Tough,
ice creams named for rockstars
and whose failed flavors earn headstones;
where the gods of the valley sleep with the gods
of the mountains, one chapel
dedicated to dead dogs.

It ain't all heaven. There's some wicked
bad history. February is too long. A skylight
helps. If it doesn't leak.

Dead Man's Hand

He built this house and died here
forty years later. He chose
the mute beige and two greens,
snow-globe sparkle lights
in the kitchen remodel.
He stacked the rock-wall paths
through mountain laurel
and kousa dogwoods. His death
stained the wall-to-wall carpeting.

What makes this mine—
mortgage? Deed?
My dogs' hair clotted
on new rugs?
What says respect
among summer solstice shadows?

I grab a buckthorn sprout
tangled in the lilac row,
lean in to cut it,
and find an old stub,
his cut. His hand
and mine aimed
at the same sapling.

When Your Begging Bowl Fills with Hailstones

After Santōka, a Japanese poet and monk
who died penniless in 1940

Days come at you like this.

Your shallow cup that leaks holds all the water
you have for a ten-mile trek home.
You get locked inside a chicken coop

with five broody hens when the latch misfires.
Yesterday's work to accomplish
five simple goals does not help you

get through today's list of ten.
Your red trowel has gone missing,
and you don't believe in ghosts

despite the overwhelming
evidence you live with one.

I Need a Virgin Mirror

—Elizabeth Bishop

Untouched silvered-glass rolls off
a conveyor belt, gets sheathed in plastic tape,
slides to a framer, to pre-formed styrofoam,
then shrink-wrapped, cardboarded,
sealed and smacked with a label
to cross the country by air.
To see only good, love, honesty?
Rear view?

Bigger than a diary, the gift arrives.
I hold it up to make a spare room
seem bigger, let it see the woods.

I run to a peace cast upon clear-water—
to minnows and mayflies,
water striders and tadpoles,
wiggles as tiny as truth, revisited
grace in a looking glass,
eye to eye on this.

In Praise of Silent Wing

We scare the barred owl
from its daytime roost,
the forester and I scuffling
through the snow and ice
to spray-paint trunks of invasives.
The owl barely has time
to take off over our heads.

I know silence. Consonants fall down
my throat as if I no longer know
my language. My deception
of being the old lady without
speech is a played-out trick,
disability of neural design.
Bungled words still gurgle up.

My forester explains owl silence
on hunt as stealth in wing beat:
mix of serrations and velvety
down fringe feathers that
suck up turbulence. And noise.

My species expects me to speak out
for truths of all that has gone
wrong for people and for owls.
I would be that creature
with wide wingspan who moves
deliberately and undetected.

Found

My new garden hides treasures
dropped and forgotten.

Tape measure, trowel, watering wand,
St. Thomas cross, a tumbled concrete boy
configured to pee from a hose.
One tarnished metal butterfly
as big as an eagle.

This morning a life-size pottery rabbit
that cracked to pieces in a freeze:
right ear, V of a nose, round butt,
and tail of potsherds I scour up,

beneath this morning's call, your news
of stage four cancer and what tests come next.

Could I make the rabbit whole with super glue?

                    Best
to leave shards in a tumble-heap
for another day, when this is again
only a once-frozen broken bunny.

Old Woman Living Alone

Wake up and open child eyes.

Sniff the incense of silence
and coffee from a one-cup press.

Melt cheese on tortillas with jalapeño salsa.
Sink into the red leather armchair.

Know messes will wait for later.

Read the instructions.

Foil. Rekey the locks.

Listen. Mice at night.

Welcome moonshine through skylight.

Accept: cardinals do not linger,
and chipmunks undermine the walk.

Squint to banish the fetch from the dog's shadow.

Keep pilot lights lit and palms open to sky.

Send postcards to old friends you left behind.

Relish dawn, then fireflies.

Never cut a memory short.

Imagine: midnight's clanging baseboard is
a schooner pulling away from a rickety dock.

Redefine sanctuary, here and hereafter.

Ask, *Who knocks at my door?*

Wonder who will never knock.

To My Postcard Collection

You don't want to hear that fleeting
word—*email*. You know
every story has two sides,
even *wish you were here, I miss you,*
or *thank you for your kindness over tea.*

You bear extra-special images of antique
roses, Wyoming's wonky jackalope,
Inuit line drawing of whales, the photos
of motorized skates or Escher's waterfall
from the Museum of Impractical Devices.

I love your flimsiness inviting
my right hand to scrawl with no fear
of the fingerprint of delete.
Go ahead—invite the mail carrier
to flip you like a pancake
destined for a drool of maple syrup.

My scribble intrigues those carriers
who approach hard-knock mail slots
and arched sheet-metal boxes, wary
of the mad dog, to sling ads
for grocer's sales or water bills.

When you drop through the slot
to the friend's vestibule floor,
go ahead—reinvent yourself,
as a bookmark in the bodice-ripper
parked beside the unmade bed.

Meditation by the Pond

My cell phone is set to chime
my end time, with ripples.

I count breath, then frogs, then breath.
  The first day—five frogs hoist onto lily pads,

a fond yardstick for stillness
  hanging in algae.

Three frogs the next afternoon.
  I miss the missing,

until a goldfinch charm arrives
  to balance on evergreen twigs,

as if I am invisible. My eyes only,
  wondering

why a dragonfly hovers in front of my nose,
  as my heartbeats slow to next to none,

and no frog leaps when ripples play.

The Newcomer Begs the Land

> We still remember the names of these places and our relations
> and we have not forgotten our own name. For those outside of
> our memory, the mission remains to bring them home. This is still
> our homeland and the bones of our ancestors speak to us.
> —Abenaki Statement on Indigenous People's Day 2017

The bones of this land are not mine.
My wary steps crack old twigs
and storm-tortured limbs, seek

delicate mushrooms and polypores
I identify from a field guide.
I find pits dug to reclaim border rocks

and hillocks-for-no-reason in the woods
of greenly trees whose name and nuts,
strangers to me, let me pass.

I see cycles of hardwoods, pasture,
and return to forest; and learn
to identify red-back salamanders,

wood frogs with their black masks.
I gather birch bark strips
upon which to write haiku.

Abenaki names twist my tongue,
Adalskiôbid, The Watcher.
Am I judged?

Ktsi Nwaskw, Great Spirit,
whose name I cannot say,
tell me who is buried here.

This forest became mine
through thefts with many names
I know.

Coming-of-Age Story

Alice: *Where should I go?*
The Cheshire Cat: *That depends on where you want to end up.*
—Lewis Carroll

I've finished with courtship, so a love affair
won't write this script. I abandoned my parent's
ashes; this won't be a generational saga.
Are deepening wrinkles and lifting dumbbells
the staples of this moving story

when little is safe or secure. Neither sex nor ice skating.

                    First Vermont winter: cocooned
in a slab house, no cellars for roots, doors stuck in frozen.
Poems about living alone. My math-whiz mind calculates
percentages of years lived in solitude. A water pipe cracks
beneath the slab.

In the left-behind place, friends said I was brave,
snow-cocky, assuming all-wheel drive would keep me
out of the culvert (it didn't). Tipped in front of revelers
inside drinking mulled red wine on Christmas Eve.

I lift a turtle to turn it for a photo,
stumble under its weight, and fall
into a rockery, learn later
snapping turtles bite off fingers.

Summer adds to my butterfly list: hickory hairstreak
and eastern blue. I plant milkweed
for the next improbable monarch,
talk to the green frog as if it welcomes me

to the pond, rather than standing guard,
see my dogs transform into avid predators—
cottontail, chipmunk, squirrel, frog, voles,
and moles.

Assume an ending of ashes.
Seek wild land near where
the hickory drops its nuts
or a cardinal sings.

Binge Writing

A woman named Hope
blogs lists of distillers,
recipes for incendiary martinis,
mezcal's history.

She says full-time writing
about booze, barstools,
and body/mind benders
pulls her further away
from alcoholism.

I get the irony—
appeasing loneliness
by scribbling postcards
about waked-up nights
or the slow gilding
of the male goldfinch.
I tuck a poem into a pocket
to touch at a gathering
where I know no one.

As I describe this valley,
pasture, peaks, or crowns
of eastern pines, a cork
slips back into my keg.

The Possible

What would happen
if there were a terrific shortage of goldenrod
in the world
—Grace Paley

Pulling goldenrod in the back garden
requires stooping and jerking.
Stiff stems rip up gloves.
Yank or wrench, my fingers throb.
This herb roots here, while rhizomes
make neighbors there.

Sweat slides from under my straw hat
—as I struggle to liberate
a white hydrangea, three blueberry bushes,
and six hostas smothered
under head-heavy gold.

The thickest stalks snap off—
even stacked they could re-root
to return like my cousins' two-week visits
during the muggiest days of August.

I work for what is possible—
ox-eye daisies, black-eyed Susans,
and blue asters
that resist temptations
of fussy hybrids.

Lo·ca·vore

noun: a person whose diet consists principally
of locally grown or produced food

Seek out poets who call your place home,
who walk your streets, observe
the fantasies and foibles
of your governor,
know when your trees bloom
or flare in flame.

Even when these poets tell stories
that may not be entirely true,
they breathe what you breathe,
make you see what they see:
crumpled Bud cans in the alley,
the bear across the pond,
a child too sad to sing,
nations flying flags on razor wire.

Accept that shelves holding up local poets
in your bookstore are short. Urge
librarians to buy their chapbooks.
Continue to read the poets (Rumi,
Shakespeare, Billy Collins, Mary Oliver)
whose words you hear in sermons,
weddings, and funerals, knowing

that reading local poets confirms
your neighbor explores lunacy, logic,
laws, leafage, laughter, lyricism,
lushness, love, and lickspittles
and braves the same snowstorms.

Poetry is never fake.
Ask the Jabberwock.

What I'm Famous For

Pie crust, light-rolled,
flaky to the edge, peach,
apple, and the mincemeat
my brother dutifully eats
because I say it's his favorite.

I'm famous for certainties—
which channel the stream will choose
after the next flood. I point a direction
squarely one way, and others nod
rather than go rounds to disagree.
I can outlast anyone on a hula hoop.

Known for sending postcards—
a panorama down the Columbia River Gorge,
a lithograph of a girl fleeing a courtroom crowd
to net a butterfly before it scoots out a window.

When I say I keep a clean house,
I don't count clots of dog hair,
sheets gone a few weeks past washing.
I mean my garden is in order,
nothing invasive chokes out the foamflower.
Walk barefoot on my paths, relish moss
on recycled bricks, drink my rose verbena tea.

I am famous for being too serious,
meaning gullible when you've lived with jokers
who tell hoodwinking stories
as if sincerity and honesty live
on one weighted side of a duplicitous coin.

I have written my own elegy.
I encourage you to do the same.
There is no knowing what people will say
if you don't say it first.

Ruth Stone

You're my who-would-I want-to-eat-dinner with.
First: your beach rhyme of *eel-grass* and *sea glass*,
then your fondness for font, type, game-piece alphabets
held in blue velvet pouches to sprinkle on paper like confetti.

Then your truths of what you knew—and I have come to:
memory becomes the exercise against loss.
The universe is sad. No one knows you.
Your grave poems flesh out tricky calligraphies:

how human cells renew themselves every seven years
but remember the old body and its love of love.
You saw yourself in the mirrors, caskets,
paintings, shadow silhouettes without dimension.

You gave us bagworms who never fly
but wait for the railroad, bus, or an assembly line
of words to take off into myth or curdled laughter.
Your galaxy accepts orbits and fleas below snowberries,

wrinkled skin, and sleep. You tell how to step
in crusted knee-deep snow, see fractals in sand,
grope for the blur of entrances and exits, know when
to board the train and when to watch it roll.

Wild Apples

Mellow gold skin
with a hot-flash blush
sprung in a wetland
where wanderers dropped seed
or where neglect overcame
a pioneer orchard. Unkempt
volunteers respected
for hardiness, serving
beyond their time.

Come September,
heavy-bearing limbs
beckon, tease the doe
and taunt the coming snow.

Wild apples.
Is this who I am?
No one's necessity
ripening
to cider—

sweet,
then tart
before it vinegars.

To David Budbill, Recluse on Judevine Mountain

People my age either retire,
count last days, or profess
that the *R* word means death.
Some *transition*.

Others travel to Yosemite
before all the sequoias burn,
send postcards from the Great Wall,
snapshots of Cinqua Terre,
share stories of brothy stews
in a room carved in a stone cave
with wood benches that scrape
slate floors. Earnest poets trek
the Camino or bicycle the Loire.
Not many chose seclusion.
What they do AC (After-COVID)
remains to be seen.

My sphere has shrunk to a deer trail
near a spring. I follow rabbit tracks
in snow to see if cottontails are loyal
to one trail from my front porch
to the failed satellite dish
embedded in a buckthorn thicket.
There I pretend to intercept messages
from outer space as poems—
the source of my reveal
that Santa is a trans-woman
known to her peers as Stella.

I prize a simple table
and peppermint tea.
A good murder mystery.
A wool hat against wind
that bites.

When I ask Google to find
a word for a woman hermit,
I get names for pet hermit crabs:
Clawdia or Shelly.

Under the Comforter of the Coldest Winter Night

(Ninety-nine percent of the words from a WinterSilks catalog,
rearranged.)

Nighttime comes in violet blue (but not dusk blue)
after black cherry, smoky purple, and later
midnight navy or black.

Just the right touches of lace say
snuggle up for sleeping in chill nights.
Your crocodile-embossed relaxed legs

must-have snowflake patterns on memory foam.
Nothing says flexible quite like a union suit:
two roomy pockets, no muffin top, unisex.

You can't go wrong when temperatures drop
because everyone needs a wash, feather-light
ease of movement, and touch with thumb

and forefinger. Especially like this.
Just the right amount. All-over smoothing.
(not shown) I'm blushing a dash of feminine,

a hint of itch-free, it's perfect alone.
And closure, crotch to hem,
fits most with love, unless noted.

Cozy like a cloud inside and out.
Forget all about the snow falling
when temperatures drop.

Pull on sleep, your silhouette
of gold violin drapes like a timeless dream,
no front or back, easy care.

Return to original condition.
The terms may change at any time.

My Daughter Meets My White Pine

> That was my woodlot; that was my lot in the woods. The silvery
> needles of the pine straining the light.
> —Henry David Thoreau

If we added together your age
and mine, this pine is older,
destined to outlive us both.
Touch its bark,
trace the puzzle pieces.
A thin maple twines beside
and up inside the pine:
maple's red-gold flaunting
its place within wind-blown silver.

You study the bowing-to-earth gnarled
branching of this wolf tree, an old one spared
to leave shade for grazers when the woods
was cleared for pasture, a century older
than other trees in the woods.

You see my sacred tree as a scientist does;
I see this as a mother.

We are not so different—
years from now, return,
to sit under one limb or the other
to remember me
after the crickets stop singing.

Sfumato

A northern Vermont skyline at dusk—
low clouds tarry on the sun's tilt
off the high ridge. Coral shades to gray.
Winter-stubbled pastures slope to ice
on the river's blurred boundaries.

A time-lapse movie could catch
linen sky dissolve to smoke,
then old bone smeared with pewter.

Inside, dusk deadens a pillow from scarlet
to wine, the chair from jam to mulberry.
The black dog blends in with her bed.
Your hazel eyes darken with tints
of ambient worry. I light the lamp.

Beyond the window, what's visible fades
to a slurry of black onyx, raven, and slate.
The glass reflects cones of sullied gold
pooling over you as you nod while reading,
halfway between sleep and waking.
I could paint peace.

Every Day Tell the Hours by the Shadows

—after Adelaide Crapsey

Evening presses December's gloom.
Snow-burdens fall on the roof from hickory trees,
drum on the skylights and smother them in slush.

Little Dog shudders, the one who fears her house
will fall to pieces if she relaxes her vigilance,
the one who later snores in my bed.

The sift of snow weights pine branches into slants.
The shadow of my hand hovers over lined paper:
a lone fist, curved hook with no eye.

My guest left today. This vacant hour piles
on top of the day's listless work: wash, fold,
sweep, stretch clean sheets, shovel the walk

no one uses. All that's left is to call the dog
from her bone, turn off two table lamps,
nod good-night to the snow-glow moon,

and walk to where my shadow sleeps.

What Does It Mean?

A New Year with this number
seems impossibly high.

In a mystery set in Quebec, the detective says life
is one big longhouse. Not a warehouse with cubicles
or industrial shelving. Never a basement with cubbyholes.
Nor a parking lot for used cars and deflated red balloons.
Huge rectangles covered in bark where nothing hides;
everything is visible. Nothing disappears.
You never leave your family.

Eight Vermont poets discuss
how to peel an apple so the skin falls
in one piece and whether it's a Yankee
tradition; whether Druids used apple twigs
as divining rods. Google found
sixty-seven million responses
about apple slices turning brown.
Starlings eat frozen crabapples.

The Moth Radio Hour notes
that Christmas always ends
and that every holiday
deserves a drag queen.

Crones

I call myself a crone to be visible
in the muttering forest
of long-held roots.

To be counted as one of those elders—
the eighty-year-old with teenage legs,
the caregiver's hands easing birthing and dying,
or she who watches from the lead-gray window
of third-floor finality, a soprano who crazed her voice.

I paint a golden mandala.
I know those who nightly light
the forgiveness lamp, despite all they know,
and wake to allow outrage to stoke the fire
for a warmer, brighter morning.

We have worn necklaces of stones, chalices,
and pearls, wiped tears from the cataracts of angels,
heard babies off in the cry room,
mothers scuttling like mice to attend.
We have been handmade.

Our skirts bedraggled, our shawl fringes
laced with remnants of rage and silence.
We stand for woolly resilience.

The best of us have studied how
to untie knots
without tugging
or breaking
a single thread.

Last Chance: New Year's

Subject lines on every request scream
these words. Text bodies detail wounds:
hungry, homeless,
therapy dogs,
coastal wildlands,
war-maimed, unheard wolves,
starving dolphins, NAACP,
election fraud, tax equity,
Greenpeace. Red Cross.
Mercury in rivers.
Your mailbox was full of these, too.

We endured these the last week
between winter holidays, and
we gave to some of them.
The doctors gave bad answers.
One friend's sister
died in her favorite chair
two hours before the party.
Bills went unpaid. Shoes wore out
or cramped the toes of the growing.
The roof leaked. We did not send
relief to Yemen.

We seek hope as if we can wrap it
like gauze around our pounding skulls.
We will do what we did
last year. Take what comes.
Speak up. Practice
kindness at every
last chance.

Stolen Color

Accept dirty-blond grass and bland peach
in a January sunset. When your home darkroom
door opened, you emerged from red light
with monochromes of razor wire fences,
old cars in Cuba, sneakers
climbing library stairs, my fingers
rubbing the wood grain of a cedar stump.
Scuffed essence. Unnamed feelings
in black and white.

Winter as we live it—
backlit, shadowed. My heart
would sing if a cardinal entered
the yard, but he doesn't. Red

stays away. Winter flaunts
a warped tattoo of twigs on crust.
So many crows hunker in birches,
and so many pipe organs of icicles
dangle in silence; I relearn stark.

The Poetry-Writing Handbook for New Year's

suggests two alternatives: decide if the phoenix
eats its old ashes or gives packets of dust
in silk pouches to adoring witnesses

who sprinkle it as hope—chances to get it right
this time around. You are allowed to list the ten
worst failures and the highlights of ten best

based on how they looked, felt to fingers, smelled—
with details of the ball slamming to a goal,
the dawn a friend died leaving a letter to be mailed.

Reach back to flame-glow on a thoughtful face
at the fireplace, having gone in for less dark
with a sip of something claret-red in an etched glass.

Make your own ashes, one heave of a vast stash
of to-do reminders, bills, poems, and letters
that went unanswered or said enough for then.

This is not a beginning, not even close,
except for babies. This is the going-forward—
maybe lusty, partly lastly, inevitably likely.

Thirty Things a Poet Should Know

you will pay for your coffee
no hat is right for every occasion
when you hear a bird call, give it a name
cows kill more people each year than sharks do
few can name the sixty-some English names for pink
death won't rhyme with health; wealth rhymes with stealth
many writers compose their best work during pandemics
your audience may hear bear foot when you read barefoot
one of the great poets wrote an ode to salt
the world's largest salt mine is 1,800 feet under Lake Huron
tears evaporate unless you catch them
when praise is needed, do not hesitate
embrace yourself as both title and footnote
learn from the wind's scansion of a noble fir in a squall
pronouns take shortcuts like rivers
a muse flows in her own stream until you build a raft
imagining Kanthaka when you read horse is acceptable
hoard matches for when the way is dark
tender your sorrows
some poets are buried under cathedrals
some are laid to rest in pauper's fields
memorize one line that an ancient said
insure does not mean ensure
once earth held more trees than stars in the Milky Way
typewriters called for two spaces after a period
rules change
the U. S. Constitution was printed on hemp
read your way to writing
what you are looking for is not lost
the moon is there, somewhere

Pagan Epiphany in the Night Woods

How easy to imagine sorcerers afoot,
studying a comet, their plunder-walk
in green robes and scarves, scooting
behind bare red oaks and ancient
sugar maples, clutching at ironwood
to steady their footsteps through drifts.

This night I would have them
search for truth in a rarified sky,
for the Dipper pouring love
to the shivering.

Three sets of footprints.
Red fox, bobcat, and doe
hold up to plummeting cold.
With what faith they cross
the road to the woods.

What do they know of each other,
of my dogs, of me? These trees
note passage, hover over
revelation of relations—
a forest king cake
of rabbit scat and trail,
frosting of moonlight.

Candles

These arrow flames waver
on one winter table
to eat at the body of wax.

If I sit still,
   the edges slump
and spill, and I smell
persimmon smoke.

I rewind the story
of my mother as beauty queen,
the way our histories burned
as she tried to smear hers
into me like blister wax
that drools down
with no clear course,

a hot history
until that snuffing day
I spoke to her lingering
coma and whispered
in her ear:
Let go, go out.

Seduction Mean as a Snake

Soft snow, inch after inch, a few hours on the clock,
a porch chair sports a downy ten-inch pillow. Each twig
grabs bragging rights to long white evening gloves
and wind-bows to the great wonder of the universe.

That's how it starts, as if winter's world is magic,
sunshine pierces the white to squints, plush
up to the wells around the blue spruce, mashed
where someone tried to walk a dog. Squished
into inches of ice on the road with so-what hashtags
from chains in a town and plows. At the bottom
of a bowl of steep hills, days upon days
of inches upon inches over the boot tops,
the little dog's cough.

Now daggers haunt my roof. Three feet
of saber rattling, overhang, danger.
The sky grays up for more ice, double dose,
freezing rain that over a day or maybe two
melts snow. After ice. Then floods.
Rivers full, over the edge,
and we see dog pee in old snow,
how the kids are all over the fun
of sledding, and everyone is out
of eggs. Housebound makes a good person
mean as a snake, come too close I strike,
or grab a roof-dagger and gut the sad-bent rhodies.

Walking on Water

Wait for ice to paralyze
the pond, for the crackling
thinness to thicken
so the under-water moans.

Scuffle through rice-snow
where slush went solid
around someone else's boot.
Hike around the hockey rink
and the men and children ice fishing
beside coolers of beer and chips.

Let the lake lure you
away from the eyes of cabins,
from smoke signals
fanning from chimneys.
January's water strider,
as small as the lake makes you
hidden in a hooded coat.

Remainder Snow

Shriveled like old
mandarin oranges
in a white bowl

or dimpled
like the white thighs of aging women
in bathing suits, those lap swimmers

who remember how they smiled
in photos when their babies' bottoms bulged.

Lone Loon on Lower Pond, Hinesburg, Vermont

The puddle in my bucket list evaporates month by month
as what seemed urgent becomes less so.
I haven't given up on monarch's overwintering
in the Oyamel forests, so many hanging chads
whose votes for life we discount.

I never give up on seeing a loon.
My daughter calls me at dusk,
to the spotting scope on her dock.

One loon,
a symmetry in black and white,
cruises the pond. Dives, surfaces,
glides through deepening darkness,
as bats arrive to whirl after bugs.
Peepers call for all they are worth.

The water lies still under a pregnant haze.
The firs across the way grow up and grow
down in reflections that do not waver
even as the loon passes across the lake.
Its red eye of summer, the mating eye,
is a minute dot.

My desire to hear its wail-flute drops
back into my bucket. My daughter
places my hand on her belly
to feel my grandson kick.
I add to my pail: to hear this baby laugh.

August Night I Sang the Twilight

Does it get any sweeter than a sunset smear of ripe peaches
over the Adirondacks, those gray slumped whales in a blue mist?
Roaming east of where Lake Champlain fills in with the blue we
once named baby, I open my car window to let fly a peppy
tune from the local radio station that I do not ever expect to hear
again. The fields hayed once this summer green up again with
milkweed, goldenrod, and chicory. I remember the sweet maple
creemee from the take-out window at the burger place. On my
passenger seat, a quart of just-picked blueberries to make a pie
for family arriving for the birthing of a grandson.

Sultry and humid,
summer's end
humming.

To My Grandson

I make lists of things to tell you. Then I get distracted by news that today the Zimbabweans ran out of paper for making passports. Or how the words *cutting edge* can apply to paper's slice of a fingertip so scissors, paper, stone is not so simple. Consider *healing* and *reparations*: different etymologies and similar meanings. If I could imagine the role of electronics in your life, I'd be a genius. I hope Tibetans will still sing songs the dead Dalai Lamas wrote.

Many things I cannot explain. One of your great-great grandfathers died in the 1918 flu pandemic; you are being raised with coronavirus, watching us wear masks.

Listen to peepers and crickets. Borrow the wings of the white crane. Revere the dragonfly. Ask your father why he lets fish go. Ask your mother why she loved mud mucking. Learn about the ten thousand things. Welcome the wood's silence.

You will witness war(s). My ancestors fought on the right side of the Civil War. My father built mobile soup kitchens deployed in World War II. I'm unsure how many men I knew died in Vietnam. Memorize a route to the border.

Accept training on tools, including your grandfather's handmade ice-fishing tip-ups. Respect that your father keeps his guns in a safe. Learn long division. Enjoy adding. Subtraction may dominate your life.

You will forget important things. Patch the leaking bucket with duct tape if that's all you have.

If you ask what I hold sacred, I'd answer: milkweed, horses, dogs, trees taller than houses, bluegrass, old stories, loons, the smell of heritage roses, a few people, poetry and songs by people who tell the truth.

I am afraid; I suspect you will find out why.

Rhytides

Someone has written a poem about everything—
pepper grinders, gravity, dandelions, Marie Curie,
black holes, Morse Code, train tracks, comets—
so why not rhytides, wrinkles that accrue interest
after slow investments: those sleep creases
or harms that make skin lax
like rubber bands too long in a drawer.

When blogs name what is written on a face,
advice turns to treatment: hydration, injections,
surgery. Physicians promise to unwrite
what stretches with the smile, frown, grimace.

I favor the truth of personal history channels
like how I slept once with a friend I hadn't seen
in fifty years on the blue side of a silk pillow.
Or ran into headwind from the north, scouring
Mt. St. Helen's falling ash into my face.

Whatever the puckered etymology,
I welcome rhythmic tides
of wrinkles that carved the becoming
of where I've been in winds, waters, and gravity.

Rowens

We are second harvests, little one,
green patches covering stubble-fields
where wild turkeys lurk. August gleaning
before we face our winters. Our nights fly over
like bats and eagles and kites—swooping
over geographies of overgrown pasture
abutting forest and ruined landscapes
my peers held dear.

You swim now muffled in womb's water.
Our days, yours and mine, will span
three centuries of flooded furrows.
How wide-eyed you'll come to first light,
dawn as a plump breast and blankets.
For you, a first tooth, first everything.
For me the certain length of another winter.

May we be useful, tender, help feed
the world's hunger despite our acres
of discontent. To ripen into the best,
we're called to be in separate seasons.

September Migration

Tattered monarchs head south over
Muddy Brook Reserve. One-way traffic.
Adults on wing over shoulder-high goldenrod,
purple and white asters. None of the milkweed
show tell-tale green and yellow-striped larvae;
too late for that. The dragonflies lack direction,
free-buzz like Harley guys out for a spin.
The monarchs aim for Mexico.

And two weeks ago a baby was born.
Transformed. Water to air. Water to milk.
Rolled up to rolled out. Thumped
to burp; new rules. Whispers
in an unbuffered ear about wanderers
changing the world. Cloud ogres wearing
pantaloons and boots.

Without my doing anything more concrete
than wishing, little one, you transform me
into a grandmother, that benevolent force
that must watch over some cocoons
to help them become monarchs.

One butterfly lands on a wild purple aster.
I reach into my pocket for a cell phone
to grab a close-up of orange and black
on purple and green. Focus. The monarch
is gone. Nothing stands still.

The course of "granding" teaches that I won't see
everywhere you go and all you will become.

So I witness and record this September afternoon
when the monarchs knew what they had to do,
differing from what the dragonflies had to do.
The day I peeled strips of birch bark to write a letter
to your grandfather. Magic is subtle. The cricket
drone is louder now than the mosquito's whine.

May your peregrinations bring you one day
to stand in a meadow like this shoulder-high
with goldenrod, smelling of gone-feral apple trees
and gray dogwood berries turning purple.

Knitting Is Coding

—Elisabetta Matsumoto

You don't have to know string theory
to know what unites yarn and knitters.
We start with straight lines to give birth
to elasticity and stretch—then loops,
coils, and intertwines, code
reverses and combinations.

Each stitch curls up in a silent wish:
the man who needs wool socks
for ice fishing and hockey, the grandma
who drapes her shoulders in purple,
a winter hat for the homeless teen, booties
a newborn kicks at a sky he cannot see.

The knitter has your back—and hands,
skull, neck, arms, and toes.
Now a baby blanket, 30" by 30"
folds in my basket to swaddle
my grandson during cool dusks
of fussiness

       while we scrutinize his eyes
and jawline to find which snippets
of whose strung genes slipped where,
how hope knitted up this particular way
to make him whole and absolutely new.

The Dead Won't Leave Me Alone

The night brings them to me in lucid dreams
I prefer to those where my teeth fall out.

Rose helps me decide what to pack
for a long trip to revisit Oregon.

She listens to the not-very-long story
about my grandson's first snot nose

and tells stories about what her grands
are up to as teenagers, still good kids.

My father merely listens; I can smell
his breath, but I guess he's been dead

so long he's forgotten how to talk,
choosing to be gentle and approve.

I'm surprised to feel their kindness.
They don't stir up nightmares;

the wrenching part is waking up
to remember they are gone.

Why Buy an Antique Mantel Clock

One that the owner says worked
thirty years ago when she last turned
the key. I have already down-sized.

Timepiece circa 1848, a gothic steeple
missing one hand. Faded instructions
glued inside on the needs of care.

Brass works, signed by clockmakers
Brewster & Ingrahams, Bristol, CT.
A clock that lurches past each minute

with pointed hands, slow progress
from hour to hour, what I once knew
to be the stuttered way time moves.

Added to my digital others, silent
like me, this one a gong that
may or may not toll reliably.

For this: to become that child again on a green
afternoon kneeling in the neighbors' den waiting
for the hour's clang as a tornado rolls over.

To go back to when I too was surer
in my movements, I use the excuse
my grandson should learn workings

of a pendulum, gears, and coils,
the see-saw of escapement
as time loosens and unwinds.

Celestial Milk

Poets have milked the moon a million times
with tug-on-udder words about slow bruises,
departed muses, the seeping loss of milkiness,
or torn-up love tossed to that pocked stone—
light reflected from an indifferent source.

We've slathered scrims over the Milky Way—
what a long way you have to go to see it spread
as canopy to the night. We no longer
steer our boats by star charts.
Most of us never knew how.
As for wish upon, believe if you must.

So for stars: grab what joy you can
from names of myth and numbers.
Accept the puzzling presence
of planets' glow. Think why
you imprisoned June's firefly
in a Mason jar and as you grew up,
you vowed to never do it again.

                                    I rest
in knowing that my grandson drinks
at the breast. His mother is his star
and this season's constant moon.
I'm a secondary, hovering Milky Way
when she must go outside, blazing
her way in a livelihood that explores
how this planet might survive.

Amabie*

*The amabie is a Japanese mermaid or merman with three legs who emerges to prophesy an epidemic.

In corona-hours, everything may be afraid of something. Spring's wind tears at the clumps of dog hair I hung up for the birds as possible nest linings. The chickadees scatter. A goldfinch bounces off the glass of my sunroom window. You'd never say the moon is afraid of the sun, maybe just dependent for shine. Today, at first light, the moon stands up in a dawn-blue sky, defiant. Another gust swirls the tops of the silver pines and blows downed hickory leaves across the yard like juncos searching seed. I am flung seed, fur dangling on a black wrought-iron fence, and a moon alive only for moments in its morning.

Coloring
the paper print-out
of the amabie.

I Might Need This

The day began with a man at a podium near a flag. Then videos of drapes going in the swinging doors and rolled out over coffins to rumbling refrigerator trucks on their way to over-filled mortuaries. Coffins arrayed in parallel lines as on a bingo board.

When I tucked cotton remnants inside the sewing kit, I thought: *I might need this someday.* Then I forgot about them.

I open that case on a closet shelf beside my first-aid kit and summer's electric fan. Acknowledge the red pin-cushion heart, a wedding gift. Peel apart fabric leftovers: gold stars splattered on black, red boats with sails unfurled. Two apron strings from my mother. The teddy bears that beared up my baby's room as curtains near the fir tree where the raccoon ate the robin's babies.

Now is that someday. A bear mask on my lips, over my nose. Filter my words. See-beyond the grisly crosswalk.

Empty streets
and stoplights
that March night.

The Purgatory of Homebound

This is not the absolute worst nor the best.
Either is imaginable, even foreseeable,
according to those who know the most,
make myth or foment lies,

but universal truths did not make it
to all sectors. The sun is white hot,
outlining the abstracts of naked winter
limbs unrecovered. Maple and red oak.

A few inches of daffodils poke up
under a chain link fence. You look
beyond the windows, through
to where the mourning doves play,

not flirtatious yet, just aware
of themselves strutting opened-up grass
the snow tamped down. Whatever
you have washed, there is more

that needs your attention, more
that threatens—a yawning cupboard,
the boxes on the porch you don't dare
open because you don't know who

touched them last. You puddle
suspicion within the sun's warmth
slanting through the window, where
the dog naps as if heaven is here.

Old stories try to guide you.
This plague is no punishment.
You need stories of people holed up
in igloos, castles, or cabins teetering

in high rocky passes, the tales
they share of where they were born,
how they lived, what they learned,
what they aspire to at the next turn

where no certain next exists
even in candlelight.

The Journey

The trip to see my grandson takes twelve minutes each way. I admire a red barn with an American flag painted on the doors, a pasture of black steers, a turn-off for a sugar shack, a wandering turkey, one bicycle rider in gold Lycra, and a sign for the farmer's market to open in two weeks with new protocols.

Steering wheel sticky
from hand sanitizer,
the smell of manure.

My grandson and his mother and father sprawl on a red blanket on their newly mowed lawn in the shade of pine trees. My daughter spreads a red-and-white-striped towel for me, six feet from the baby. The baby, clothed only in a diaper, knows my face. He burbles something remarkably like hi, drawn out and guttural. I admire everything he does: his ability to sit up without falling over, to pull on his mother's t-shirt to get himself standing, to turn the pages on a cardboard book to his favorite page with pictures of goats, a horse, and two dogs. I do not move off my assigned towel. He rubs his eyes, nap time. Going home the other way, I pass four fields of young corn for the market stand.

My kingdom
for a horse
to brush its mane.

Blue

Blue seeps from my eyelids to form up
with my waking—morning fog-lidded
Blue; my old friend, the familiar who
lurks on the pillow like a cat might
if I liked cats. She can buff up
into cornflower, seldom babyish, and once
cosmic, a jolt. Her edginess rains down
on me like haughty laughter.

I feed her reds like anger
and love to try to turn her purple,
but it never works, neither do beets.
Pinot nor cranberries. Her demeanor
is both comfort and tease. I know denim.
I know sky. I know the dark nights
she does not like; she says stars
broadcast all the fluorescence possible,
and she will not compete. She is never
midnight. Her refusals storm at me.

So we move along with each other,
side by side, mostly complicit.
Misty blue and ambling me.
Lapis and loneliness.
Lavender and luck.
Periwinkle and possibility.

Alonely

You endure it as sands of allotment,
gritty and abrasive.

You know how much you can allow
like coins stolen from the cookie jar.

Allege is for schemers. Allure
for anyone who looks better in a mask.

Alumni makes you realize
how many friends have died.

The alarm sounds shrill,
alternately far away and then

aligned with worry.

Messages

Memo is too formal. To-do list demands action.
  My missives lie between hint and whisper.

Linnaeus made a clock out of the intervals
  when his marigolds opened and closed.

A message he could read. What I stir into the dust
  on the mahogany chest under the broken clock

is not laziness, the spiral suggests memories
  of Stonehenge and zodiacal lions.

My survivors won't know how much to feed
  the dog or why I kept the doll's head.

Lining up my will, instructions for the dogs,
  passwords and numbers—those are concretes

beyond the unnecessary details of where the sun
  comes through the window at 4 pm,

how much the living room darkens when snow
  settles on skylights, why I held a funeral

for the rugged sugar maple
  that fell over in the storm,

two centuries
  of twisted giant laid to rest alone.

Questions

How much closure can you expect
from sewing on a button?

If your fingers find loose threads
on your tapestry, must you tie a knot?

When you travel in circles,
do you measure the distance,

or what you know now
that you didn't know then?

Have you watched
children's games in cemeteries,

hide-and-seeks, alphabet games,
romps their grandparents forgot?

What rules determine
when a happy ending is true?

Why the cruciform power poles
lining roads and the hand-balanced

rock walls at pioneer graveyards—
to keep them in or us out?

Who will end in dirt,
who in flame?

Which where emerges
at the end of when?

NOTES

Li Po epigraph in "No Home on that Range" is from *The New Directions Anthology of Classical Chinese Poetry*, edited by Eliot Weinberger, New Directions Publishing, 2003.

"I Need a Virgin Mirror" is a line from Elizabeth Bishop's poem "The Riverman."

Epigraph to the poem "The Possible" is from Gracey Paley's poem "Goldenrod" in *Begin Again Collected Poems*, 2000.

Ruth Stone poetry lines: "No one knows you" is from "At Age Eighty-Three She Lives Alone" in the book *In The Next Galaxy*, Copper Canyon Press, 2002. Other lines are from Stone's *Simplicity* collection, Paris Press, 1995. She was the 2007 Vermont State Poet.

"To David Budbill, Recluse on Judevine Mountain:" The Vermont Legislature posthumously acknowledged Budbill as The People's Poet of Vermont after his death in 2016. Much of his poetry focuses on living a quiet life in Northern Vermont with nods to the reclusive Chinese poets of centuries ago—an inspiration to this poet living alone in isolation during the COVID pandemic.

"Every Day Tell the Hours by Their Shadows" is a line from "Sundial," a cinquain of Adelaide Crapsey's, Verse, Alfred A. Knopf, 1934.

Elisabetta Matsumoto is a mathematician and physicist at the Georgia Institute of Technology whose article "Knitting is Coding" appeared in the New York Times on May 17, 2019.

TITLE INDEX

A

B

C

D

First Line Index

H

I

L

M

N

U

W

Y